GRANT WRITING SCHOOL

PROVEN HACKS TO WRITING A WINNING AND SUCCESSFUL GRANT FOR NONPROFITS.

Aretha Janine Simons

GRANT WRITING SCHOOL

Proven hacks to writing a winning and successful grant for non-profits

©2022 by Aretha Janine Simons
Published by Multiplying Talents International, Inc.

ISBN: 979-8-9867885-1-7

To request permissions, contact the publisher at multiplyingtalents@gmail.com
Arethasimons.com

In Memory of

Doretha Clemons Simons

WANT TO KNOW MORE ABOUT GRANT WRITING

SCAN NOW

Join us

GrantWritingSchool.org

|CONTENTS

CHAPTER 1:
INTRODUCTION

Nonprofit organizations are facing difficult times. Government and foundation grants are becoming scarce. At the same time, the number of agencies requesting funding and residents in need of services are growing. The moment has arrived for grant writers to devise fresh grant writing tactics.

So you've decided to write a grant. Perhaps you don't want to submit a grant, but you and your colleagues have concluded that it is the best way to complete a critical project. If you've never written a grant before, the procedure might look pretty frightening. Perhaps you've read horror stories about spending months figuring out the grant environment, its vocabulary, and procedures before ever beginning to create an application. Or perhaps you've heard the typical refrain of grant writers: "We never truly had a chance, given the volume of applications."

Traditionally, grant writers requesting cash from government or other agencies wait until they get notification from a funding source that funds are available. This notification is known as a Request for Proposal (RFP), and it includes guidelines for applying for money as well as a deadline. Grant writers looking for foundation money could visit the library or a number of Websites to get a list of foundations that offer funds in their geographic region and for the services they provide. They can then mail applications to those who appear to provide the finest financial options.

Invariably, the "due date" for submitting grant applications does not offer enough time to prepare thorough and well-written grant proposals. A fresh strategy is required. Instead of waiting for the perfect RFP or discovering a potential foundation to submit to, grant writers could create a "generic" comprehensive grant for their entire organization.

This technique is practical because, while each RFP appears to have a distinct structure, they all want the same essential information:

- What are the needs of the citizens that the agency serves?

- ✎ What are the program's objectives?
- ✎ What services will be provided?
- ✎ How will the program be assessed?
- ✎ How much money is being asked for?

The establishment of the "generic grant" should begin with a study of the community's requirements for the services provided by the agency. Whether the organization delivers social assistance, the arts, recreational possibilities, or other needs, it must conduct research on the residents' needs for these services. A survey might provide this information. Interviews with current or prospective clients may be beneficial. A new strategy for gathering this information is the organization of focus groups.

After determining the needs, the following stage is to estimate the cost of each prospective activity or program. It would be critical to know, for example, which activities are several hundred dollars and which are several thousand dollars. The nonprofit organization's board of directors would then review the needs and expenses, as well as select priorities.

The charity would then start making judgments about where to apply for funding. In certain cases, the agency would seek for funding to run specific initiatives. The agency would then augment grant funding with monies raised through special events or yearly fundraising drives.

When the "generic grant" is produced and an RFP from a government agency is received, the organization will be able to fulfill deadlines more easily because most of the wording and budget have already been written. If funds become available for a day-care facility, for example, the agency will have previously assessed the demand for one and will be aware of the expenses of running one.

If a nonprofit has identified a need for six distinct programs, it can search the foundation directories and apply to one foundation for one sort of program and another foundation for another. There is also no ban against applying to several foundations or government organizations for the same monies, so that may also be a possibility.

When a potential funding source for a certain sort of program is found, the organization that has previously examined the demand for that type of service and explored the cost will be well ahead of all other agencies asking for the same monies.

CHAPTER 2:
GRANT WRITING EXPLAINED

Grant writing has earned its own aura in some areas. We want to disprove the myth that grant writing requires a master's degree. You can prepare a good grant proposal if you have common sense, time, and energy. The first step for a fresh grant writer is to believe in their abilities.

Approach grant writing in the same way you would apply for a job, as we've all done. Assume you're looking for a teaching job. You look around to discover who is recruiting in your expertise area in the districts or areas where you want to work. You discover a business opportunity that you want to explore. To acquire the position, you should learn everything you can about the school and district to which you are applying. Do they share your educational philosophy and values? Are they compatible?

You must create a cover letter and résumé that best portray who you are and are in line with the job description. You want your application information to be written clearly and arranged in an easy-to-follow and comprehend fashion. You argue that they clearly want you for the position, not someone else who may appear to be similarly competent on paper. And, just in case you aren't chosen for this position, you send your application package, with small changes, to a few other districts that appear to be a decent, if not ideal, match.

Consider the following. You'd want to obtain financing to launch a new program in your school district, such as an after-school education program for struggling pupils. You conduct some research on comparable initiatives, how they are funded, and who is sponsoring them. You investigate the groups that appear to be interested in assisting with this type of activity. Which one appears to be most in line with your project objectives? Where is the ideal match? You create a grant proposal that clearly articulates your need, project concept, and how you will show and quantify success. Using the basic criteria provided, you want your project to stand out as the best at meeting the funder's needs. And, if this donor does not choose your idea, you send your application to a few others, modifying it to meet the parameters specified by each.

Writing a good grant is similar to applying for a job in that you want to portray yourself clearly and effectively as the best choice in both circumstances. In each scenario, an interview may be required before a decision is reached. In essence, the methods are identical and simple. Use the tools, ideas, and information in this chapter, to assist you navigate the grant creation process and improve your chances of being chosen as the best candidate. You've got this!

Grant Terminology: Sign Interpretation

You can't go far in grant writing if you can't read the signs. The area of grant writing, like education, law, and health care, has its own vocabulary. So, let us begin our journey into the land of grants by learning the basics of the language.

What exactly do we mean when we say "grant"? A grant is money or other resources provided to complete a specific project. A grant is the prize or reward that you seek to support a project that you want to see through to completion. Grants are provided by organizations or agencies that are interested in implementing specific types of initiatives and have the necessary resources. These organizations or agencies usually offer funds through a competitive procedure, which means that people apply, their application packages are assessed, and only the best ideas are funded.

Grant awards are sometimes used to refer to monies awarded to assist successful initiatives. The actual grant award contains the grant amount and the time frame for using grant funds. Grant awards are sometimes accompanied by a set of additional specific requirements pertaining to the usage of the funds awarded.

Someone chasing a grant, like someone looking for work, is an applicant. You may be applying for a grant as an individual, on behalf of the educational authority you represent, or (more commonly) on behalf of a partnership seeking and securing financing for a project. As an applicant, you must follow a formal application process that is set by the organization or agency receiving the grant funds.

The organizations or entities that provide grants are known by a variety of names: The phrases grantor, financier, and grant maker all refer to their position in the process. Throughout the book, we use these phrases interchangeably. Grantors can include federal or state government agencies or departments, as well as foundations representing companies or private groups.

A proposal or application is the form of grant information that you send to a potential donor. In the context of the grants procedure, these phrases are also interchangeable. Grant applications often include a standard set of components that define the who, what, where, when, how, and why of your project. A budget for financing the work to be done is frequently included in the proposal, as well as a description of how success will be measured.

A proposal discusses in full your desired project and makes the argument for why it should be financed.

Finally, but not least, your proposal is usually produced in response to a Request for Proposals, or RFP (or less commonly, a Request for Applications, or RFA). This is a grantor's invitation to submit an application or proposal for financing. RFPs are covered in depth in the next chapter.

CHAPTER 3:

GETTING TO KNOW "REQUEST FOR PROPOSALS" (RFP)

The most popular grant acronym is RFP, which stands for Request for Proposals. This is an offer from the financier to "ask me for the money" or "show me your proposal." Almost all grant awards, or monies awarded in response to a successful proposal, begin with a thorough examination of an RFP. The RFP outlines all of the information you must include in your application to be considered for funding. It also defines submission and delivery timeframes for your proposal. It may include formatting guidelines for creating your proposal (such as margin width, line spacing, and font size), mandatory attachments (such as letters of support, staff résumés, promotional materials, and fiscal reports), and other important information.

Most RFPs have a standard set of components, but each organization's RFP will have its own unique elements. Almost all donors will seek answers to the following questions:

- What is the project's concept? What does it have to do with your mission? What about ours?

- What is the significance of this initiative, and what needs will it address?

- What are the project's objectives? What are the expected outcomes?

- What activities will you engage in to achieve your objectives?

- How will you know whether you are succeeding? What methods will you employ?

- How much will the project cost? How much assistance do you require from us?

- Who else is involved in the project, and how are they involved?

- Who are the key individuals and partners responsible for carrying out the project? What are their credentials and experience?

If the initiative is successful, how will you continue to support it in the long run?

KEY DETAILS TO REMEMBER

Grant writing is a direct and doable process that you can accomplish successfully.

Understanding the basic terminology of grants is important for moving forward.

Grant funders may be federal, state, or local agencies; private foundations; or corporate foundations.

Understanding the differences between possible donors is critical when determining where to apply.

The RFP is crucial to the grant development phase, and all RFPs have a key characteristic.

CHAPTER 4:
KEY FACTS BEFORE WRITING GRANTS

So you've identified a possible donor, the issues your project addresses align with the grantor's goals, and you've began to form alliances with others to make your effort a reality. It is now time to start writing. Most calls for proposals and grant application packages share a standard set of components, however the sequence and title of these might vary. Completing an application, or creating a good proposal, entails paying close attention to each area and writing exactly in response to the instructions supplied by that specific donor or grantor. This may seem apparent, yet funders frequently complain that the great majority of proposals they get do not contain the necessary information in the proper location.

Debbie Rey, who oversees the W. K. Kellogg Foundation's proposal processing office, estimates that 80 percent of grant applications that come across her desk are instantly denied. "They may have glanced at the Web site but did not explore deeper to uncover Kellogg's precise grant-making priorities," she claims ("Grant Makers Reveal," 2003).

"Your request should be crystal clear and demonstrate how programs fit exactly within donors' goals," says Karen Murrell, Fannie Mae Foundation senior director of outreach and education. "Conduct research. Most applications are rejected immediately by Fannie Mae because they fall outside of its financing criteria" (CD Publications, 2003).

Read a Successful Grant Proposal

One easy suggestion, especially for those new to grant writing, is to find an excellent (that is, funded) submission and thoroughly read it. And here's a helpful hint: Read it with the RFP to which it was written. Comparing each RFP heading to the actual answer from a successful candidate may be highly beneficial.

Obviously, repeating this practice with several grant proposals and RFPs will expand your understanding of what grant reviewers consider to be good. It will also provide you with some comparative information on topics such as writing tone, data usage, how applicant organizations articulate their strategic alignment with funders' priorities, examples of management and partnership structures, budget construction in relation to project design, and so on.

Where can you find examples of good proposals? Inquire with colleagues or organizational partners about grants they have received and ask to review them. Contact educators from other districts who have received grants comparable to the ones you are looking for. Most individuals are happy to give examples of their accomplishment as long as you are not competing for the same financing sources. As examples, several grant contests include copies of winning bids. If you identify a grant program that is relevant to the type of project you want to sponsor, contact the funder and get copies of successful bids. You may also find (typically online) additional projects sponsored by the donor or the RFP that you identified. Request a copy of the winning candidates' application packet from them. Rebecca acquired a copy of a successful 21st Century grant application from colleagues in the district where she was formally employed when a local district with whom she works was pursuing a 21st Century Community Learning Center award. Most individuals are eager to offer this knowledge since they already have the money and do not regard you as a competitor.

Avoid Making Blind Submissions: Establish Contact with the Funder

It's natural to want to be supportive of individuals you know and like. This fundamental idea may also be seen in the process of requesting for and obtaining funding from "friends" who represent federal or state agencies, corporate or private foundations. Making a personal connection with someone representing the funding source can have a beneficial impact on grant award choices.

Another method to consider developing a connection with a specific donor is to ask yourself, "How can my proposal stand out from the potentially hundreds of others that are similar when it comes down to making the difficult choices?" One answer is that if the grants officer, board trustee, or other individual involved in the review process knows something about you—your integrity, qualifications and experience, commitment to truly making a difference in your community, thoroughness in addressing the funding agency's interests—you and your project can rise above the pile of good proposals.

We no longer submit proposals to potential funders without first initiating some type of human contact as a matter of policy. You should do the same, utilizing any of several methods. One easy method is to contact or email a designated grants officer in charge of the grant program in question. (Calling is preferable than e-mailing since it is more personal and allows you to show your interest and passion more readily.) Read the RFP carefully and conduct research on the funder, searching at things like instances of past giving, grant award levels and geographic distribution, current goals, and the language they use to describe their objectives. Use this information to craft intelligent questions that connect your project concept to their RFP. Make sure to include your name and the name of your company in your e-mail or phone call, and repeat it at the conclusion. Mention some of your partners if you have the opportunity. Demonstrate your commitment to working together to fulfill a genuine need.

Another option to establish a personal connection is to ask a grants officer or other funding representative to evaluate a basic idea draft of your project. The goal is to provide you with critical input on your proposal, but perhaps more importantly, you engage the funder directly in the development of your product. In a way, you become collaborators in the development of the idea and future proposal. Funders are more inclined to fund a project that they helped to build in order to satisfy their interests and requirements. Private and corporate foundations have more leeway in developing personal connections, but all grant programs, including federal and state agencies, are overseen by individuals who want to make a change.

Need to write a grant?

Because time is always limited, the choice to write a grant must be made first. Here are some points to consider:

Make a grant application:

- ✎ To run initiatives that your board is completely dedicated to.

- To give services where there is a demonstrable need.

- To continue initiatives that have shown to be successful.

- To run projects that have the potential for multi-year funding.

- When the chance arises, form partnerships. Many funding sources emphasize the importance of collaborative programs.

Do not apply for grants:

- To fund programs, unless you are certain they can be implemented effectively.

- To "balance the budget" in a particular fiscal year.

- To hire permanent staff, unless other sources of funds are available to continue the positions once a particular grant has been completed.

- Unless the present staff is totally committed to implement the program if it is funded.

Steps to Follow Before RFP

Before approaching government organizations or individuals with requests for proposals, approaching companies to seek for funding, or browsing foundation directories for grant possibilities, grant writers should follow these steps:

1. Needs analysis

Conduct a thorough needs analysis of the population in the covered region. Among the methods used to determine what services residents want include surveys, interviews, town hall meetings, and focus groups.

2.Strategic strategy

Create a strategy with attainable goals to satisfy the demands of the people. Time-based planning is required. List the goals that must be attained during the first year of financing, the second year, the third year, etc. The goals must be quantifiable. For instance, a goal can be "to create 50 units of low-income housing," "to put three new stop lights on Main Street," or "to provide an average of 100 meals a day to elderly residents."

3. Exercises

With as much detail as you can, describe the activities that will be offered. Include things like activity calendars, training program lesson plans, procedure manuals, and equipment descriptions.

4. Job descriptions

Include thorough job descriptions for each participant in the program's personnel. List the tasks in the order that they will likely take up the most time. For instance, an activity that will need 15% of an employee's time might be put after a task that will require 50% of that employee's time.

5. Evaluation procedure

Establish a procedure for agency-wide evaluation. Who is involved in the process (for instance, board members, employees, and clients)? What primary assessment methods (client interviews, attendance, exams, etc.) will be used?

6. *Budget*

Establish a costing strategy for each task. What will the expenses for each program's employees, equipment, leasing fees, etc. be?

The key to securing grant funding is cooperation.

When a grant is granted, showing collaboration is a key element in improving the likelihood that you'll be awarded one.

This collaboration may take a variety of forms:

- **A community's many service-providing organizations can collaborate.** One application may be submitted on behalf of a number of senior citizen facilities, AIDS prevention or treatment initiatives, or mental health organizations.

- **One can create public-private partnerships.** One option is to propose a collaborative crime-fighting plan that involves both the local police force and social service organizations.

✎ **A focus on intergovernmental collaboration is necessary.** Programs that involve participation from the federal, state, and local governments, or that entail collaboration between numerous municipalities, are more likely to get funding.

✎ **All collective communal activities ought to be highlighted.** The likelihood of receiving money is increased by submitting a program that incorporates members of the business sector, members of religious institutions, and social service groups.

Paying a visit to the financing source's representative

Most grant writers don't communicate with a representative of the funding source before submitting their applications. A face-to-face encounter with a staff member from a government agency, a trustee or staff member of a foundation, or a representative from a company would be very helpful in this fiercely competitive market. Benefits of such a conference might include:

- You would have the chance to inquire about specifics in the grant application that your rivals would omit.

- The representative of the funding source will feel more confident in your agency's capacity to manage programs as you discuss your initiatives.

- You may learn more about the funding source's unique goals and areas of interest.

- When choosing between numerous grant applications, the initiative you took to go to the funding agency could be useful.

You will have the chance to ask a number of questions that will significantly impact how you compose your application, such as:

1. How much time should go into the application?

Inquire specifically about the duration of prior funded applications from the funding representative. When a three-page application would have been funded, why prepare a 30-page application? On the other side, a 10-page plan would have been accepted, so why submit a three-page application and not receive funding?

2. Why are the monies being provided by the financing source?

Examine the legislative background that resulted in a financial allocation, for instance, when submitting a grant application to the government. Obtain the financial instructions from the donor before applying for foundation money. When requesting funding from companies, request a list of the kinds of projects they support.

3. How much money and how many grants will be given out?

If you can get this knowledge, it will be really useful. A government agency frequently has a specified budgetary allocation for a certain program. Numerous firms and substantial foundations choose certain priority areas and specify the number of awards or the range of grant amounts in each priority area.

4. Do you have access to documents of grant applications that were approved the year before?

An examination of existing proposals that have received financing may be the greatest predictor of the kinds of funding applications that will be successful. There is a compelling case to be made that government organizations must give copies of grants they've previously financed to you (the taxpayer). You should be allowed to examine prior grants, even if you might be required to analyze the applications at the agency's headquarters or pay for duplicates. A list of previous grantees may be provided by the government agency in some cases, and you may then get in touch with them to ask for a copy of the application.

A list of the previous year's donations as well as several other details about the foundation and its grantmaking procedures must be provided by foundations by law. Foundation directories, which are available at the library, include lists of grants. Major foundations frequently have a website where you may learn a lot about them.

Request a copy of the application from the organizations that the foundation or the government agency has financed. Even though it might be challenging to get beyond grant listings from firms, many annual reports and corporate newsletters do contain a list of grant awards.

5. Who decides on financing and what are their qualifications?

Knowing who will read your grant application is crucial while you're drafting it. You won't need to clarify every phrase if the reviewers are very knowledgeable in your subject. But frequently a foundation trustee or a company representative on the Allocations Committee won't have any expertise in your area of expertise. Then you will need to properly describe each technical phrase, spell out every acronym, and provide a layperson's explanation of your services.

Meeting with the person who will decide on the funds is also beneficial. If a foundation employs paid personnel, the employee will offer detailed suggestions regarding who should be financed. It is crucial to request a meeting with the person who founded the organization if they are still alive. Make an effort to meet with the donor's spouse, kid, or grandchild if they are deceased. When submitting an application to a government agency, make an effort to speak with a mid-level employee who recommends financing to a department head.

6. What standards will be applied in choosing award recipients?

How to write a grant might be greatly influenced by the selection criteria. Because they only have a limited quantity of money, many grantor organizations may choose smaller donations. Others will choose based on non-monetary criteria and haggle over the proposal's price.

Some organizations utilize "scoring sheets" to determine grant awards. A range of points will be awarded to the grant's "needs" and "budget" sections, respectively. The applicants with the highest point totals are then awarded funding. Getting a copy of the scoring system, if the agency employs such a "objective" approach, might be crucial for securing funds. When drafting the grant, you will be able to clearly identify where to put your attention.

Should you include letters of recommendation?

Getting endorsement letters from pleased clients, other agencies you work with, and political leaders takes time. The representative of the funding source should be questioned about the possibility of using these letters to determine financing, though. In addition to letters of support, a call from a senator or representative might ensure financing; conversely, it could also jeopardize funding. Therefore, knowing in advance which calls might be useful may be a crucial financial factor.

CHAPTER 5:

MASTERING THE COMPONENTS OF A GRANT PROPOSAL

The funding provider will frequently provide a Request for Proposal (RFP). When submitting a grant application, you must provide answers to these questions. Observe the directions exactly. Get formal approval from a representative of the funding source before departing from the RFP in any way. However, if you are not provided instructions, the following structure may be applied:

Table of contents, summary, introduction, need, objectives, and methods are all provided together with the cover letter.

Evaluation Appendices only for substantial grants in the budget.

1. An introduction

- On agency letterhead, draft a brief cover letter addressed to the grantor agency employee whose name, title, agency name, and address are accurate.

- Contains a brief summary of the plan in one sentence.

- Specifies the number of participants, employment attained, or additional units that the award will support.

- The entire amount of money asked is listed.

- Gives contact information for the agency's representative, including their name, postal and email addresses, and phone number.

2. The contents page

- Funders don't read grants from beginning to end, the way one would read a book. Funders might wish to go at particular aspects, such the goals or the budget. The grant writer should make it as simple as possible to find particular grant portions.

- ✎ Each page should be numbered sequentially. Put all of the page numbers on the same page (for example, in the middle of the page at the bottom).

- ✎ Provide a thorough table of contents. Every section of the grant can thus be found by the grant reader. Include an overview of what each appendix contains (for example, Appendix 4– Letter of Support from Senator John Jones, pg. 42).

3. Synopsis

A summary may be useful to the funding agency for larger grants. Keep the summary to one page or less. Other than the length of the grant, whether or not to include a summary is determined by whether or not the grant is innovative. If you are writing a grant with novel and exciting ideas, a summary may help you get funded. Many grants, on the other hand, may not include novel ideas. If yours falls into this category, you may opt out of including a synopsis.

4. Introduction

Include critical information in this part that will not appear anywhere else in the grant application. You might add the following items:

- The mission of the agency.
- The number of years the agency has been delivering the service covered by this program.

A brief history of the organization.

Significant evidence indicate the agency can run programs efficiently and successfully.

If the proposal includes eligibility conditions, a statement stating that the agency is eligible to receive the funding. A declaration of nonprofit status under Internal Revenue Code Section 501 (c) should be presented. The majority of NGOs are tax-exempt under Section 501(c) (3).

A collection of letters of support from previous clients, representatives of partnering agencies, and legislators. (The actual letters should be attached to the application as appendices.)

A statement outlining how the agency intends to support the program at the end of the grant period. This is a crucial section. If you are requesting for equipment, for example, keep in mind that no further funds will be required. If you're looking for a staff position, explain how you plan to get more funds. Perhaps this is a fee-free pilot initiative, and if successful, you will charge a price for the services.

5. Need

For a grant to be granted, the organization must show the community's need for the service to be delivered. What is the scope of the need, and how is it documented?

The need mentioned should be the need for services of persons in the community, not the need of the organization. Estimate the number of people who require counseling services rather than saying, "We need a counselor since our agency doesn't have one" or "The government slashed the money for the counselor we had."

The requirement should be for the coverage area. While national or statewide numbers may be provided, if the agency serves a specific county. An estimate of the county's need should be supplied.

There should be a need for the specific service to be provided. If the agency, for example, provides services to victims of domestic violence, the estimated number of victims of domestic violence, rather than unemployment data or other relevant statistics, should be provided.

The requirement should be quantified. How many people are expected to be eligible for the specific service supplied in the coverage area?

Common data sources include:

- **Data from the census:** Make careful you utilize up-to-date census data.

- **Counties have planning commissions:** To discover the phone number for the planning commission, contact your county commissioner's office.

- **Governmental organizations:** Excellent data sources include the Departments of Education, Health, Labor and Industry, and Welfare. Each county may have offices for the Board of Assistance (Welfare) and the Bureau of Employment Security (Labor and Industry).

- **Municipal governments:** Local police agencies are great places to get crime statistics, and local school systems may give educational material.

Data created by oneself: In many circumstances, an agency may offer the required data from internal sources. Among the sources are:

- A waiting list.

- Letters from prospective customers asking a service.

- Information acquired from surveys distributed to current clients asking them to name alternative services they might be interested in.

- Letters expressing dissatisfaction with the absence of a certain service.

- Participation in public hearings.

- Community polls.

6. Goals

The program's objectives are the planned outcomes.

The following characteristics should be present in objectives:

- ✎ **Time-based:** How many people do you think will engage in your program during the next three months? 6 months? A year?

- ✎ **Measurable:** How many people do you expect to engage in your program? Because all targets are estimations, choose a particular number, "We expect 125 people will engage in the program," you say.

- ✎ **Realistic:** Make up objectives that cannot be met if the program is financed. Keep in mind that if the funding source finances your program, the aim you specified may become a legal obligation of the program.

- ✎ **Countable:** If you get funds, ensure that the information needed to measure the objectives can be accessed. Do not include objectives in your proposal if obtaining the data to measure them would be difficult or impossible if the project were financed.

7. Procedures or activities

In this part, sketch out the program. Include the following six W's of program writing:

- **Who?** Who are the customers? How are they chosen? What are the limitations (such as age, income, and geographic location)? Who are the employees? Include a job description and a statement that outlines the education, experience, and other employment criteria when asking financing for new staff employees. Include a CV and a biographical summary for each staff member when appealing for money to keep existing employees.

- **What?** What kinds of services will be offered? Include a course overview for educational programs. Sections of an operations handbook that are relevant may be included. A story is appropriate for other programs. It is appropriate to outline the services. Others may offer a "day in the life of a customer."

- **Where?** Where are the services going to be provided? Provide the addresses of all main and branch offices. What sort of space is sought if new space is obtained using program funds?

- **When?** What hours and days of the year will services be provided?

- **Who is it?** What other organizations supply services? Include agencies that link people to service providers, for example. Describe the organizations to which you recommend your clients. It is critical to collect letters from other organizations confirming any links you claim.

- **Why?** Why is your organization offering these services instead of others? Is the agency taking any novel ways to service delivery?

8. Evaluation

Inform the funding source that the services to be given will be evaluated.

Who will be involved in the review process? Outline how board members, staff members, clients, experts in the relevant field, and community representatives will participate in the review process.

What will be assessed? List some of the concerns that the evaluation team will take into account. For example, assessors would consider if the need was reduced as a result of the services provided. Were the goals achieved? Were the services supplied in the manner described in the procedures section? Will an outside firm examine the budget? Otherwise, who will audit the payments and expenditures?

What kind of evaluation will be given? Describe how the program will be assessed in as much detail as feasible. Include the pre- and post-tests used to evaluate the classes if formal classes are given. Attach a copy of the client questionnaire to the application if one will be utilized. Explain how the program data will be examined during the assessment process. Include a description of the audit or the procedure for reviewing the budget items.

9. Budget

Inquire with the funding provider about the level of financial disclosure necessary. Many financing organizations, for example, may merely want the whole amount you intend to spend. Most government entities, on the other hand, demand a line item budget that contains a precise estimate of all money to be spent. A budget of this type might include:

Personnel expenses

- Salaries
- Fringe advantages -
- Consultant

Non-Personnel Expenses

- Travel
- Space costs
- Equipment

as well as contract services

- Consumable items
- Other expenses

Matching grants are available. Matching funds are required for many awards. A match of up to 100 percent is possible. Frequently, the request for proposal just mentions the match criteria without going into detail about how the match might be computed. Contact the funding provider and inquire whether the match must be in cash or "in-kind." If a "in-kind" match is allowed, the following budget items might be used to total the required match:

✎ **The expense of all volunteers for the program.** Use the fee that the volunteers would charge if they were paid. If your board treasurer is an accountant, for example, include the regular cost the accountant charges for his or her services as part of the matching funds.

✎ **The market value of other donated services.** If the agency, for example, does not charge leasing charges in the program, the in-kind match should include the fair market value of the leased space. If the grant staff uses the agency's computer, the in-kind match should include the cost of renting that computer.

10. Appendices

Each proposal should contain many sorts of letters of support:

✎ **Letters from prospective clients** A letter from an individual seeking the service might be useful in documenting the necessity for a certain service. A letter from a parent who need a childcare program in order to find work, for example, may be highly beneficial.

- **Letters from cooperating organizations**
  Cooperation among agencies is beneficial in receiving financing. A letter from an agency head who is willing to send clients to your organization if money is secured might be beneficial.

- **Political leaders' letters** Include letters of support for specific initiatives from federal, state, and local political leaders. Request that the elected person be as explicit as possible in describing how the program would benefit his or her neighborhood.

Looking for grants

The search for grants may start after all the data has been obtained and input on the grant writer's computer.

What financial sources from the federal, state, and local governments could have grants available to fulfill the needs of the people that agency serves? An excellent place to start could be the Catalogue of Domestic Assistance at www.cfda.gov.

Which foundation profiles best meet the demands of the population? Starting with **www.foundationcenter.org** is a wise move.

Which local companies may be encouraged to participate in the agency's service area?

Meet with the senator and congressman from your state and inquire about the particular financing options available for your program.

In your local district, arrange a meeting with your congressman or congresswoman or a member of their staff to learn more about certain federal funding sources.

Most funding providers have a website where you may get information about their programs and how to apply. The whole RFP may frequently be downloaded.

Ask for a list of their funding sources from organizations that are comparable to them in your neighborhood or in other communities.

The grant writer should then obtain an RFP or any other funding request instructions from each possible funding source that are not available on the funding agency's website. The grant writer would next go over the material from the Internet again to determine what information belonged in which particular grant applications.

For instance, a grant writer may submit a grant to a government agency to obtain cash to rent space for a school if there is a demand for an after-school program to teach computer skills to pupils. One option for funding the purchase of classroom materials is to ask a foundation. The school may invite nearby companies to provide computers and software in exchange for staff members who would teach the pupils how to use the computers.

CHAPTER 6:
UTILIZE RESOURCES TO FIND FUNDERS

Here are some useful places to start looking for possible grantors for your project. To facilitate access, each has its own Web site. The first section includes general sources of grant information, while the second is primarily focused on education.

Sources in General

Information about Federal Grants. **http://www.grants.gov** is a relatively new comprehensive online portal for looking for grants via all government offices and departments. As a potential grant applicant, you may use this site to look at all of the grant opportunities available via the federal government and refine your search using different search parameters (such as grant release time and areas of interest) to meet the nature of your project. A word of caution: if your search criteria are too restricted, you may lose out on similar chances.

Candid formerly known as Foundation Center. This website includes a massive quantity of foundation information; the site provides a variety of free and paid search possibilities. FDN Center (**http://fdncenter.org**) **https://candid.org**

GrantStation. The GrantStation website includes thousands of foundation information and sample proposals. **http://grantstation.com** You can get a huge savings on GrantStation membership with their partnership at **http://grantwritingschool.org**

GuideStar. This website provides financial information about foundations and charities, including IRS tax returns. It also has a searchable database and pay-per-click search possibilities. **https://www.guidestar.org**

Digest of Philanthropic News The Foundation Center's weekly news service is a compilation of philanthropy-related stories and features selected from print and electronic media outlets around the country. Education-Specific Resources **http://fdncenter.org/pnd/**

Forecast of Funding Opportunities from the Department of Education This page covers almost all of the programs and contests for which the Department of Education has solicited applications for new awards, as well as those that they intend to announce at a later date. It gives real or expected deadlines for submitting applications to various programs. The listings are in the form of charts that are arranged by the department's main program offices. Please keep in mind that this material is just for informational purposes and is not an official application notification from the Department of Education **https://www.ed.gov**

The Forecast of Funding Opportunities is one of numerous useful links on the Department of Education's Grants and Contracts page. Other links take you to materials such as "Grantmaking at ED: Answers to Your Discretionary Grants Process." **http://www.ed.gov/funding.html**

World Education Grants Center This website is routinely updated with a "featured grant" and a list of additional current awards. It also offers grant authors advice and resources.

Eduref.org. This online directory for education librarians includes a grant page with connections to numerous grant-related sites as well as reports, publications, and online forums for grant writers. **http://www.eduref.org/cgi-bin/res.cgi/Educational_Management/** \sGrants School Funding Center eSchool News This website offers current information on grant programs, funding sources, and technological financing. FastWEB.

http://www.eschoolnews.com/resources/funding/ With 600,000 scholarships totaling more than one billion dollars, FastWEB is the largest online scholarship search accessible. It gives students reliable, up-to-date information about scholarships, grants, and fellowships that are appropriate for their objectives and credentials, all at no cost to the student. Students should be aware that FastWEB sells student information obtained through their website (such as name, address, e-mail address, date of birth, gender, and country of citizenship). **http://www.fastweb.com/** Federal Educational Resources for Excellence (FREE). In 1997, more than 30 federal agencies organized a working group to make hundreds of government financed teaching and learning materials more accessible. The FREE Web site is the product of that effort. Fundsnet **https://fundsnetservices.com**

This is a comprehensive Web site dedicated to giving information about financial resources accessible on the Internet to charitable organizations, institutions, and universities. Grants Alert is available at **www.fundsnetservices.com.** Grants Alert is a website that assists organizations, particularly those involved in education, in obtaining the cash they require to continue their critical job. Grant Writing Tips: **http://www.grantsalert.com/SchoolGrants** has prepared an outstanding collection of guidelines for individuals seeking assistance in drafting grant bids. **https://grantsalert.com**

Resources for Healthy Youth!

This page, which is part of the National Center for Chronic Disease Prevention and Health Promotion's website, includes a link to a Healthy Youth Funding Database. The database offers information on financing options for adolescent and school health initiatives from both federal and private sources.

School Finance Center: The School Funding Center is committed to assisting schools in locating every funding source accessible in the United States.

To view the center's comprehensive grant database, a paid membership is necessary.

http://www.schoolfundingcenter.com/index.asp

Grants for Education This page contains materials and advice to assist K-12 educators in applying for and receiving special grants for a range of initiatives. **http://www.schoolgrants.org**

Get Grant Information Sent to You

You'll like having good grant information provided straight to you once you've become engrossed in locating and obtaining it. Here are a few techniques that can do this.

SPIN Search is a paid service provided by InfoEd International **(https://www.infoedglobal.com/products/spin-global-suite/)** that gives grant information such as grantor contact information, program descriptions, eligibility requirements, regional limits, and award range. Once you've defined your areas of interest and chosen keywords to specify your searches, the site will deliver this information directly to your e-mail address. Although this is a paid service, your district or agency (or a partner organization) may offer a membership through which you can obtain useful grant information.

You may set up a free e-mail service through **www.grants.gov,** the previously stated comprehensive government grant source. You can specify the funding agencies and grant categories that interest you. When new federal grant listings that fit your criteria are added to the site, the site will notify you.

There are several thematic interest area list servers on the Web that you may subscribe to for free and that feature grant information. In each issue, PEN NewsBlast (**http://publiceducation.org**) provides education news articles as well as information on particular grant possibilities and links to general sources (including many of those mentioned above).

The National Center on Secondary Education and Transition's NCSET News

(**http://www.ncset.org/enews/default.asp**) provides information particular to students with disabilities, such as funding opportunities, forthcoming events, and published materials.

Check with your colleagues and professional organizations to see if there are any additional resources that may be pointed your way.

CHAPTER 7:
PROVEN GUIDELINES TO WRITING A WINNING GRANT

W rite from the passion that sparked this whole thing. As if you were speaking to someone in person, write as if you were. Don't be concerned with numbers or specific titles. Don't be concerned about spelling, grammar, vocabulary, or any of the other "rules" we were taught in elementary school. The goal of this initial draft of the story is to depict the simplicity, harmony, and potential.

✎ Use internal abbreviations to keep the keys clicking and the internal editor at bay as you compose your initial draft. While you will not use acronyms in the final paper, use them extensively in the initial draft. Create your own shorthand for terms and phrases you know you'll use frequently. At the end of the day (when you're checking Spell Check's messages), just use your word processing program's "find and replace" editing tool to make the necessary changes.

✎ Make note and highlight any errors or changes by inserting a lengthy dash (_____), with your name initials (AJS), or another symbol to return later to fill in the blanks when you realize you have the information however can't find it readily or don't want to break the flow of writing. Again, a simple search command will identify your notes to yourself, allowing you to add the necessary information.

✎ Don't bother counting words or pages. Yes, when you submit your proposal, you will be constrained to a strict page length, but don't worry about it until later in the process. It is more vital to include what you want to express than to modify from the start. Even when rigorous trimming is required, it is considerably easier to cut pages than to add them. However, if you're used to drafting a 25-page proposal for a federal grant and the criteria change to limit the pages to 12, don't try to cut and paste a previous submission. Starting from beginning is easier, and the narrative will flow more effortlessly.

Revising Is Writing

Recognize that you will need to read and revise this paper several times. You will tweak a few things each time you reread it—and each time you ask someone else to read it. Expect to do this, and you'll have the tight, well-crafted letter of inquiry or proposal story you're looking for. If you anticipate to complete a project in a single marathon session, you will be sadly disappointed.

You may have more or less revisions than I have, but don't forget about editing.

- ✎ Emphasize the Velcro words and phrases. These are the phrases that pop out at you and stay with you. These are the terms that the reviewers will recall. Look for terms you'd like students to write down on their score sheets.

- ✎ Keep track of the flow of your emotions. Do you sense the communal conflicts described in the requirements section, or are you bored by numbers? When you read about the proposed project, do you become excited? Do you perceive the agency's steadiness, or do you detect hints of trouble? Read slowly and scribble down your feelings in the margins as you experience and alter them.

✎ Identify locations of misunderstanding where further information is required. Look for jargon, extended phrases, vocabulary with more than three syllables, and thoughts that veered off course. Check for any items you left out that should have been included. Make margin comments with a different pen or highlight them in a different color than the Velcro text.

Use the information from this initial criticism when you return to your computer to revise your first draft. Emphasize the Velcro words you want to preserve and soften the ones you don't. Duplicate words should be removed. Rewrite clumsy sentences. If a written sentence exceeds three lines, divide it in half. Use 10-cent terms instead of dollar words. All variants of the verb "to be" should be replaced with action words.

Seeking Outside Opinion

This is an excellent moment to request that everyone who provided first versions read the proposal. Encourage students to read the entire paper using Sheila Bender's three-step technique, then return to the area they are most familiar with to verify for factual correctness. It's also a good idea to have someone from a completely other field read it and give you their thoughts, especially on specific locations.

They don't get it. Even if you're requesting funds for an obscure section of nuclear biology, a layperson must be able to understand your request since someone with merely a passing acquaintance with your specialty may sit on your review panel. A banker, corporate executive, or lawyer is an excellent reader for ideas for social services. They will not be afraid to inform you if your idea is too unclear or "touchy-feely."

✎ Edit and rewrite once more. Use the input you got, but don't allow outsiders influence your proposal's course. You're want clarity, not program design. If the evaluator insists on using technical jargon you don't understand, try to strike a compromise. If the banker thinks the facility rental has to be quadrupled, perform some additional market study. However, if the program director wishes to replace guest performers for a drumming circle, keep that information in mind for your future proposal.

Proofread! Keep Spell Check open at all times, but repair errors at the end of each day to avoid disrupting the flow of your writing. Before you tell anyone else what you've written, read it out to yourself. To/too/two and other typical Spell Check errors will frequently pop off the page. However, as a last stage, this is better assigned to another individual. You'll have read the words so many times that you've virtually memorized them, and you'll read what you intended to say rather than what's on the page. If you have the time, have many sets of eyes proofread the final document.

Basic Writing Skills Are Required

Although your primary focus should be on topic, basic norms of spelling, punctuation, and sentence structure must also be observed.

- **Use jargon and acronyms** sparingly unless they are required by the funding agency. Write as though your reader is just faintly acquainted with your field of study. If you must use jargon, explain what it means the first time you use it in simple English. The same holds true for acronyms, especially when used to shorten the name of your company or project.

- **Change up the structure of your sentences**. Keep phrases and paragraphs brief. Let us reiterate the recommendation to trim sentences that exceed three lines in half. Similarly, if you come across a paragraph with more than eight typewritten lines, try breaking it up into smaller chunks. A corollary is to use active voice, which is more succinct than passive, and to make a positive message rather than a negative one.

- **Employ graphics.** Use bullets and numbered lists regularly since they are the most fundamental ways of condensing information and providing diversity to the page. Duplicate your organizational chart and program logic model. Consider using charts, graphs, infographics, and other visual components to convey the narrative of the identified requirements, program activities, and budget rather than telling it. These devices actually take up less space than they take up and are frequently easier to use.

✎ **Use thesaurus only when necessary.** Funders want to see the terms they carefully selected for their mission statements and funding goals used, therefore avoid using synonyms. However, alter the terms you know you use frequently and convert complex concepts into basic English.

✎ **Mind your language.** Although there are many jokes about our fixation with politically correct language, it is necessary to be careful with word choice.

✎ **Will the individuals who will utilize your services be participants?** Members? Clients? Subjects? What about the youth? Students in grades K-12? Children between the ages of one and five? Choose one and stick with it.

✎ Instead of battling with he/she variants, **use plural pronouns.**

✎ **Keep in mind that folks have a handicap or a medical condition.** It does not define them. Instead of "diabetics," use "clients with diabetes."

✎ **Use superlatives sparingly.** You want to build a vivid image of the necessity for your endeavor, but don't go too far and depict a Dickens scene. People who have restricted earnings are not forlorn, miserable, forgotten, unhappy, immoral, or vegetating. And, while your program is deserving of support, I doubt it is spectacular, one-of-a-kind, ground-breaking, or awe-inspiring. You're drafting a grant proposal, not a toothpaste advertising, and terms like these put doubt on your character as a serious professional.

✎ **Pay attention to the beginnings and finishes of sentences.** Never begin or conclude an idea on a low note. Put powerful sentences at the start and conclusion of paragraphs and sections. Strong words should be used at the beginning and conclusion of sentences. Find a better term every time you encounter "this," "it," or another ambiguous word.

Steps to completion

The Devil lurks in the most unexpected places, so double-check your changes/writing. Check if numbers have the right number of zeros. Keep an eye on your cutting and pasting to ensure that everything moved where you intended it to. Above important, ask again and again if your words address the questions posed by the funder. Remove the colored formatting instructions you generated at the start and go to the next phase of creating the whole proposal package.

CHAPTER 8:
SUBMISSION OF DOCUMENTS

Once again, the RFP or guidelines will specify how the donor want to receive the submission package. In this stage of the procedure, there are only a few things to be cautious about.

- ✎ **Verify the address**. It is typically obvious whether the application is to be delivered electronically or by mail, but double-check the address because some funders have several addresses for different purposes. This is especially true for federal grants where the RFP can be seen on Grants.gov but the proposal must be submitted to a specific agency or department.

- ✎ **Shun Procrastination**. Some funders accept dated time stamps and allow for Internet waits, but do not rely on them. All funders are strict about meeting deadlines, and you don't want your hard work to be undone because you were two minutes late. You'll be OK if you submit your proposal a week to ten days before the deadline.

- **Hold pages together using paper clips rather than staples**, and don't bother about fancy covers and bindings if you're submitting hard copies. Proposals are frequently disassembled and pieces distributed to various groups of individuals for assessment.

- **Double-check everything** before sealing the packet or pressing the "send" button. You double-check a postal packet to ensure that everything is included and in the correct sequence, and you double-check an online application to ensure that every blank is filled. You know that if a computer detects a blank space, it will reject the file, so fill in the blanks, even if it is an explanation of why this does not apply to you or information repeated from the line before. Examine the material's visual appearance to ensure that you didn't triple space when you meant to double space and that the uploaded copy matches the version on your computer screen.

Getting Ready for an On-Site Visit

Before making a final choice, some foundations, particularly local family and community foundations, might wish to visit your location to witness programs in operation. This is an excellent chance to establish a long-term connection and demonstrate the success of your job, but it must be approached with caution.

CHAPTER 9:
BEFORE SUBMITTING THE GRANT

When you've completed your grant application, do the following steps before shipping it to the funding source (with enough of time to fulfill the application deadline):

- Is there any industry jargon?

- Is it necessary to spell out all abbreviations the first time they are used?

- Have you followed all of the Request for Proposal (RFP) instructions?

- Is every word spelt correctly? Remember that the computer's spell check simply informs you if the word you're typing is an English word, not whether it's spelt correctly or grammatically accurate.

- Is it enjoyable to read?
- Would you finance it if you were the grantor agency?

CHAPTER 10:
LET'S MAKE A
PROPOSAL PLAN

We live in a world in which everybody is in a hurry, and that's no different when you're trying to operate a nonprofit organization. In fact, most small nonprofits are run by people who work full-time jobs, operate their nonprofit, and seldom slow down or take time to research. The sad part of it all is that many of those who are in such a hurry don't have a solid proposal plan for their nonprofit's future. When you are in urgent need of money for a program, things always look much worse than they are, so I encourage you to deliberately, purposefully, set periods of time in your schedule for research.

I believe that if we research and have a plan of action- this will be the victory over complaining and short falls. Spend several hours on a weekend researching grants or donation opportunities or hire someone to do some research. This valuable research is important to the success of your nonprofit's financial growth. If a weekend is not possible, did you know that you can do more in 30 minutes than you could if you did nothing? Did you know if you do nothing, that another nonprofit is doing the research and will keep on going if your nonprofit is not around?

The "bottom line" is – do some research. I want to leave you with an exercise to try and is my Grant Writing Proposal Plan Method.

> *The Grant Writing Proposal Plan method is the fastest, easiest way to write a grant proposal. Using key words and short phrases, proposals can be created for multiple grants, projects, or programs…on a single page. This methodology focuses everyone in your organization on what is important and critical for success!*

The hidden power of gaining financial support is the ability to infect others with the why? Too often people are exciting with the ideas of starting a nonprofit, all the ideas are written in journals, typed in emails, on your phone, but if you want someone to understand that web of ideas from your mind, you've got to find a way to get it into something more concise and succinct. Putting your ideas into a proposal plan is the first step. It will force you to break down the nonprofit into each area so you can articulate those areas or components clearly. I read someone where and I cannot quote who wrote this because there was no name by it but it was an old cliche from investors:

If you want advice for your nonprofit, ask for money. If you want money, ask for advice. To succeed, you will need both. You owe it to yourself and anyone you meet to have a description of the vision, mission, objectives, strategies, and action plans ready in a moment's notice.

Let's begin our proposal together, learning how to tell your story so that we can be champions for our cause and keep the interest of the reader.

The Grant Writing Proposal Plan method is the fastest, easiest way to write a grant proposal. Using key words and short phrases, proposals can be created for multiple grants, projects, or programs. This methodology focuses everyone in your organization on what is important and critical for success!

I recommend you start your proposal with a short story or a quote to catch the grant reviews attention or bring them into your thought process as to your why. Use this as a guide to help you start with your plan.

CHAPTER 11:
GRANT WRITING PROPOSAL PLAN METHOD

What is the long term vision?

_____

_____

_____

_____

_____

Why does this nonprofit exist?

What is your purpose or mission statement?

_____

_____

_____

_____

_____

What will you measure?

What community and target market do you serve—who are they?

_____

_____

_____

_____

_____

_____

_____

What is the work to be done?

Briefly describe your current program activities

_____

_____

_____

_____

_____

_____

_____

CONCLUSION

In conclusion, I want to keep in mind that a grant is a gift. As you are using the gifts to take care of your community, make sure you take time to take care of yourself and stay healthy. Join us at grantwritingschool.org

Best wishes and Happy Grant Writing!

ACCESS TO GRANT STATION DISCOUNT USING OUR CODE

Save 60%

SCAN NOW

Follow these steps to get your discount

1. Visit GrantWritingSchool.org

2. Click on the link for GrantStation Special or https://grantstation.com/product/GWS

3. Create your account with GrantStation.com

4. Once you're done, start finding your funders.

www.grantwritingschool.org

WANT TO KNOW MORE ABOUT GRANT WRITING

SCAN NOW

Join us

GrantWritingSchool.org

HAVE QUESTIONS
OR NEED HELP PREPARING
NONPROFIT DOCUMENTS?

SCAN NOW

Contact Us
MultiplyingTalents.com

Made in the USA
Coppell, TX
11 September 2024

37067014R10048